SANTA ANA PUBLIC LIBRARY

D0754376

EUROPE

Go Exploring! Continents and Oceans

By Steffi Cavell-Clarke

©This edition was published in 2018. First published in 2017.

Book Life
King's Lynn
Norfolk PE30 4LS

ISBN: 978-1-78637-056-3

Written by:
Steffi Cavell-Clarke

Edited by:
Grace Jones

Designed by:
Natalie Carr

A catalogue record for this book is available from the British Library.

All facts, statistics, web addresses and URLs in this book were verified as valid and accurate at time of writing. No responsibility for any changes to external websites or references can be accepted by either the author or publisher.

EUROPE

CONTENTS

Words in **red** can be found in the glossary on page 23.

WHAT IS A CONTINENT?

A continent is a very large area of land that covers part of the Earth's surface. There are seven continents in total. There are also five oceans that surround the seven continents.

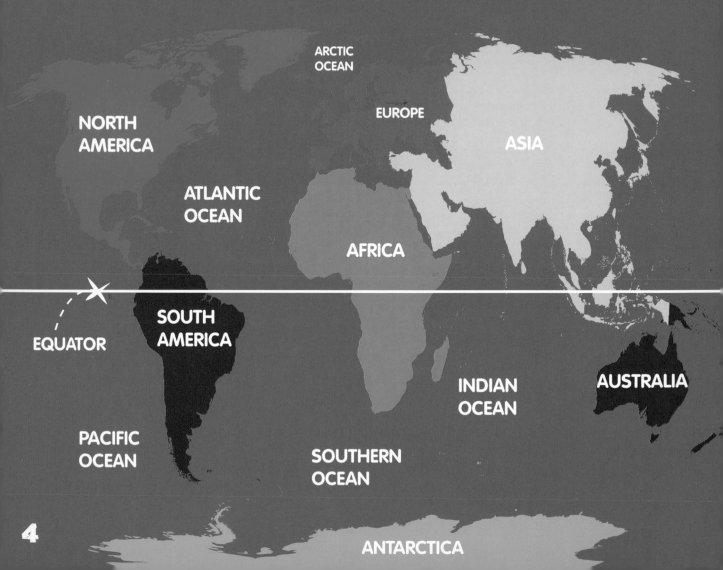

ARCTIC
OCEAN

EUROPE

ASIA

NORTH
AMERICA

ATLANTIC
OCEAN

AFRICA

SOUTH
AMERICA

EQUATOR

INDIAN
OCEAN

AUSTRALIA

PACIFIC
OCEAN

SOUTHERN
OCEAN

4

ANTARCTICA

The seven continents are home to the Earth's **population.** Each continent has many different types of weather, landscape and wildlife. Let's go exploring!

WHERE IS EUROPE?

Europe is **located** to the north of Africa and to the west of Asia. The western side of the European continent is surrounded by the Atlantic and Arctic Oceans. The eastern side of Europe is connected to Asia by land.

London, England

Arctic Ocean

Europe

Atlantic Ocean

N
W   E
S

The European continent includes many countries and over 100 islands. Islands are areas of land that are completely surrounded by water.

Area of Europe:
10.18 million square kilomatres (km)

Edinburgh Castle

Stonehenge

Great Britain

Population of Europe:
over 742 million

OCEANS

A sea is an extremely large area of saltwater. The biggest seas in the world are called oceans. Just like countries, seas and oceans have different names.

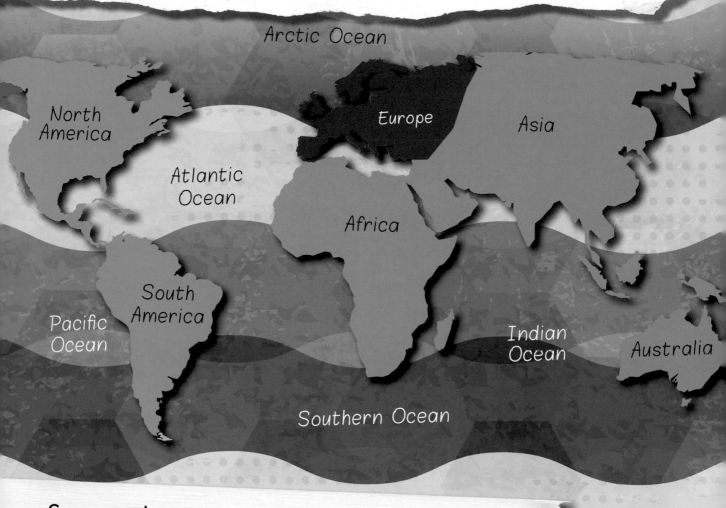

Arctic Ocean

North America

Europe

Asia

Atlantic Ocean

Africa

South America

Pacific Ocean

Indian Ocean

Australia

Southern Ocean

Seas and oceans surround most of Europe.

FACT FILE

Atlantic Ocean:
Area: 15% of Earth's surface
Average Depth: 3,339 metres

Arctic Ocean:
Area: 2.8% of the Earth's surface
Average Depth: 1,038 metres

Depth is how deep the water is.

Arctic Ocean

Atlantic Ocean

COUNTRIES

There are 50 different countries in Europe. Russia is the largest country in the world, but only part of it is included in Europe.

Iceland

Denmark

Netherlands

Russia

United Kingdom

Sweden

Norway

Finland

Estonia

Ireland

Belgium

Lithuania

Switzerland

Germany

Poland

Belarus

Ukraine

Moldova

Portugal

Czech Rep

Austria

Slovakia

Hungary

Romania

Spain

Italy

Serbia

Bulgaria

Slovenia

Bosnia & Herzegovina

Albania

Cyprus

Croatia

Montenegro

Greece

Macedonia

FACT FILE

Largest Landmass	Russia	Largest country in the world
Most Populated City	Moscow, Russia	Over 11 million
Famous Landmark	Eiffel Tower, Paris, France	300 metres high
Highest Peak	Dykh-Tau, Russia	5,205 metres high
Smallest Mammal	Etruscan Shrew	4 centimetres long

WEATHER

The **climate** in Europe changes across the continent. It is colder in the north and becomes warmer towards the **Equator**. The Equator runs along the middle of the Earth, which is the warmest part of the world.

Colder

Hotter

Equator

Hotter

Colder

Madrid, Spain

The European continent has four different seasons. The seasons are winter, spring, summer and autumn. The weather changes in each season. It becomes colder in the winter and hotter in the summer.

Winter

Summer

Winter:	December, January, February
Spring:	March, April, May
Summer:	June, July, August
Autumn:	September, October, November

LANDSCAPE

There are many different types of landscape across Europe. There are lakes, forests, mountains and many **coastal** areas.

Each landscape has its own physical features, such as vegetation.

The Alps are Europe's highest mountain range. They stretch across southern and central areas of Europe and are mostly covered in ice and snow. This long **mountain range** is home to many different types of vegetation and wildlife.

The Alps

The highest peak in the Alps is Mont Blanc, which is 4,810 metres high.

Agriculture has a big impact on Europe's landscape. Almost a third of the land in Europe is used for farming. Wheat is the most common crop grown in Europe.

Wheat

Sea Beds

The seas around Europe spread out into large oceans. Under the surface of the oceans there are sea beds that are covered in sand, mud and rock. The sea bed has an uneven surface just like land.

WILDLIFE

Europe is home to many different types of animal. Wildlife can be found all over the continent.

Crab

Hedgehog

Squirrel

Deer

Bumblebee

Frog

Lizard

Fox

40 cm

The red squirrel is usually around 40cm long
and eats nuts, berries and seeds.

There are many **species** of wildlife that live in
woodland areas across Europe. Some of the most
common animals found in these areas are foxes,
deer and squirrels.

SETTLEMENTS

Millions of people in Europe live and work in large, busy cities. Some of the largest cities in Europe are London, Berlin and Madrid.

Population of London: Over 8.5 million

London, United Kingdom

Berlin, Germany

Madrid, Spain

Some people in Europe live on farms in the countryside. Farmers grow crops that are often sold to the local markets. Farmers also raise animals, such as cattle and sheep.

Cattle

Sheep

THE ENVIRONMENT

In the large cities, people produce a lot of rubbish and waste which can cause **pollution**. This can harm humans and wildlife.

We can help to save our environment by recycling our rubbish.

GLOSSARY

agriculture the practise of farming

climate the average weather of an area

coastal near to a sea

equator imaginary line running around the middle of the Earth

located where something can be found

mammal an animal that has warm blood, a backbone and usually has fur

mountain range a group of connected mountains

physical features things on earth that have been made by nature

pollution something that is harmful to the environment

population number of people living in a place

species a type of animal

vegetation types of plant found in an area

woodland an area of land covered with plants

INDEX

PHOTOCREDITS